VOL II: The Radical Poetry of Karl Omar Lawrence

Karl Omar Lawrence

VOL II: The Radical Poetry of Karl Omar Lawrence
1st Edition
Copyright 2019 by Karl Omar Lawrence

All rights reserved. Except as permitted under the U.S. Copyright Act of 1976, no part of this book may be reproduced, distributed, or transmitted in any forms or by any means, or stored in a database or retrieval system, without prior written permission of the author.

ISBN 978-0-578-45831-1

Cover Design by Cristian Reyes
Book Design by Cristian Reyes
Editorial assistance by Lisa Schamess, Sam P.K. Collins
Printed in the United States of America

Dedication

To William "Sunni" D. Harper

"it is better to light a candle than to curse the dark, and when the apple is ripe it will fall from the tree."

Dear Karl,

    I appreciate you, my friend, for who you have been in my life in over just a short amount of time. I hope you know that as an artist, especially as a writer, sometimes you won't see the immediate return of the seeds you plant. This doesn't mean, though, that they are any less real. While I pray continually that you see the richness of your impact and that generations of people will associate you with your profound work, I also leave open all the wonderful ways that people who you may never meet, people living worlds away now, will be sparked by your imagination. Trust that as a writer, or, "builders of the world" as my good friend calls them, your projects are working mightily behind your back and under your nose to accomplish your intent and some. As an artist, your art will grow and live unpredictably.
    The first letter I received from you came during the time I mentioned on the phone when friends who I never thought would turn turned. For the first time in my life I had made serious enemies. I took your words then as a sign to continue with strength. They, as much as anything, are what helped me to walk bravely through the path that was ahead. The words I have wasted since then bemoaning the absence of that insignificant crowd would have been better spent mirroring the faith that you put into me. More than anything, please forgive me for this; I was not then as attune to seeing the horizon beyond the immediate wreckage. I commend your bravery then and now, friend. It reminded me to be braver.
    Since courage seems central to much of what we're talking about lately — the bravery to not run from the pressure of adversity, believe beyond circumstance, and make the road by walking — I wanted to share a few thoughts on the subject which we have only surfaced indirectly thus far. I don't believe that true courage is ever fully void of fear. Courage, in my estimation, is the ability to act bravely in the face of fear, not to be immune to it altogether. People are at our best, though, when they channel all of their fear into something more positive than their minds want to accept is possible or likely.
    The presence of fear caused by the possibility of failure is what, in essence, keeps any creative endeavor honest enough to bring forth magnificent art. The quote you recently sent me speaks to this: "When you have sank lower than you ever have before you will rise higher than you have ever climbed, because the exigencies of the situation will demand that much from you." I sense that we are both in familiar territory where it feels every day that we will either sink or swim. While I want to leave room for the in-betweenness of this predicament and the mysterious presence I have always felt that provides for me (and I suspect for us) no matter what; I also know well enough to listen to our instincts when they are speaking to us with such urgency.
    The worst we could do during this time is panic. The most faithless posture, after all we have made it through, is obsession over deficit. If we are left with nothing but the shirts on our back, then it's time to go forward and make a world from those shirts. Much more will come in due time. I sense in my heart, as you do, that you/me/we are destined for a great future. So this is not an ode to the false humility of growing comfortable with lack. It's a strategic suggestion from years of learning that building starts with using what is available to us in the most useful ways possible, putting everything of good nature to use and even using that which has previously worked against us as our own agents. One step at a time, one win at a time, focusing on what we can control.
    All in all, my brother, I am thankful that in this moment I have a brother who is as soundly committed to me as you have been. I share this commitment with you. I am here if and when you ever need me. From my end, what has helped me most in our dialogues is this tendency of ours to believe together beyond the current circumstance. This kind of courage has a generative effect that compels me to be brilliant. I hope it does the same for you.

Warmly,

Anthony Grimes

imagine

now imagine
a mass of matter and energy
condensed into a single point in the blackness of space
that suddenly exploded
out of nowhere
in a big bang
nobody knows why this all came to be
the table of elements doesn't tell us everything by itself
that's why ever since the beginning of civilization
we've been filling in the gaps
looking up at the sun moon and stars
trying to connect the dots of our cosmos
wondering what else is out there beyond the walls of our intelligence
how can we be confident that this existence isn't all just a dream
with no meaning outside of what we create in our conscious minds
what if
it is possible we are all alone in a galaxy that
constantly expands
it's uncanny how from fragments of atoms and molecules
light
water and gas
emerged our beautiful blue planet earth
full of complex organisms
ecosystems of living things
bacteria
plants animals and algae
imagine
a human animal evolved alongside chimpanzees in east africa
both man and woman
african american asian and european alike
a part of one united species of homo sapiens
underneath all made of the same stuff
despite what we may think
the

minor differences in skin pigment are no big deal
culture aside
we really are not that different from each other or from the apes that we lock
behind cages in zoos and train to do tricks
yet and still we are
if only
by a little bit
but what a difference that little bit of dna does make
because it gave us a brain
capable of amazing things
gave us the gift of speech language and imagination to see a possibility not
there and make it real
a ceaseless curiosity
that would lead us across deserts and ocean seas
inspire us to create things and make stone tools
master the use of fire
learn to survive in the wild
in a lost land long before recorded time
when we lived in tribes of hunter gatherers
mostly peaceful and egalitarian
can you imagine
man and woman
before marriage and private property
when we were eating fruits off of trees
could breathe deep the air
drink from streams of clean water
living carefree
spending all day
making love in the green grasses
way back
before greenhouse gases
imagine travel without a passport
no borders or war
no countries to kill or die for above us only sky
imagine a time
before agriculture and the permanent settlements that segregated us into

separate sections and classes like
rich and poor
black and white
stories invented to cement hierarchy
turn villages into cities and build empires
pyramids
bridges
aqueducts and coliseums
imagine
writing and money
what would keep it all together throughout history
laws and religious scriptures all came from the same place
buddhism islam and christianity
the inquisitions and crusades of the catholic church
death to the infidels said the pope
let us pray
but pass the collection plate
if you ever expect to get into heaven you've got to pay for it
demonstrate your faith
imagine how many millions lying dead in the dirt over their interpretations of
words written by goat herders
worms have no priests or archbishops and can't imagine man's inhumanity to
man
once a common animal
a naked savage
crisscrossing the atlantic and the pacific with maps of the globe
telescopes and the scientific instruments that would give rise to capitalism
imagine
the white man never colonized this planet what would life be like if christopher
columbus died sick on his ship
cortez never step foot in the new world with gifts of smallpox and infestation
for the american indians telling them they were from an inferior race imagine
the slave trade
the start of racism the rape of an entire continent imagine the african
whose hands once established some of the world's first universities forced to
work in fields like an animal at gunpoint

fearing the crack of the whip from a racist cracker just because he was black
back full of marks and scars
whole families on the auction block like livestock traded like cattle and sheep
brainwashed treated worse than dogs beaten into submission until we were
weak to make sure we grew the wheat and pick the cotton
mistreated
excluded
used and abused for hundreds of years without pay
generation after generation in school they don't teach you that it was
blood sweat and tears that funded the first major american companies
paved the way for the industrial revolution that put electricity in city skylines
and took us to the moon
no
the history books all say that the slaves were happy
it was the white man's burden
manifest destiny
an education made to manufacture robots for the manufacturing plant
with no imagination
imagine we tell our children
you can't be a dancer or an artist quit imagining things
that's how we kill our sons and daughters from the inside
get them ready to be sent to the assembly line from the age of 5 years old
pledge allegiance to the state
slave for the market
is it any wonder why they won't talk to you at the dinner table
are you even able to imagine life beyond a 9-5?
how did we arrive here?
atom bombs
diagrams of distant planets
maps of the genetic code
information
superhighways
no time for family
stuck on the highway
hiding our loneliness in the glass faces of phones and apps
on facebook but afraid to sit face to face and look each other in the eyes

imagine you had to put it down
could you
experience life in real time
imagine real life and not a highlight reel
imagine
if it was okay to talk about your feelings
be real and not be seen as weak
imagine connection
what if empathy was a class we all had to take and you'd be laughed at if you
were selfish
imagine compassion
imagine rapists had to switch places with the women they assaulted
imagine women were not taught to depend on men and expect them to spend
money
imagine we were all feminists
teachers got paid more than basketball players
imagine you couldn't be famous unless you were really saying something
imagine prisons made to rehabilitate
universal basic income
no bombs
take away all the guns
imagine a young man
alone and afraid
transform into a radical
of contagious passion and unmatched talent
charismatic and ambitious
whose mission was to get you to reimagine the status quo
imagine his name was karl with a k from the bronx
born to poverty premature in an incubator not expected to make it but i
survived by a miracle the doctors couldn't explain
i aint making this up
imagine the pain of my coming of age in a place where teenagers claim sets
household full of conflict sickness substance addiction
clouds of cigarette and marijuana smoke
roaches and rats
eviction notice on the door

city marshal with the chainsaw
tryna make rent from loose change make food stamps stretch
imagine the stress and the pressure of being born with less
trapped in
wage slavery with no escape we never took a vacation
i still remember the day
they sent me home from school
we couldn't pay tuition
my mom asked me if i could trade in my videogames
only options looking like a job at the post office
robbing
or serving fast food
you couldn't imagine
a nigga like me
came straight from the eye of the storm
an outside from the inner city
but my vision is different
tell you the truth
i aint been the same since i met malcolm x
saw the stars reflected in the night sky that's when i made my mind up
that i was gon see what this life was all about for myself
i said it
on the steps of my tenement sunni said it
when we met on the train
that the pen and the paper would take me places
make no excuses
it's up to you
take this serious
he believed in me helped me to see that i was great
k
you are a genius seize your destiny
get out of the ghetto grow a movement
faith moves mountains
imagine
my transition from the rooftop of my complex to mountaintops in foreign
countries top floor looking down

look how a book took me to a limited liability company
getting money on the books
independent no limit
big boss rich radical
maps and affirmations on my wall
master plan i made it happen!
the stepping stones to a self-made self-educated success who took the staircase
the elevator was broken!
hopeless homeless and jobless
but still stayed persistent
came a long way
then i came back to show you how dreams manifest
sitting back
reminiscing on how it all happened
manuscript on my desk
imagining libraries and schools
that could teach these lessons
to other people like me
you may say that i'm a dreamer but i know
i'm not the only one
who can imagine.

.

money

now everybody wants to be happy but when is it ever that simple
ask anybody
you can't just be happy
you've got to have things
and since you can't get something for nothing you need money
money
the answer to all of the problems you have
access is granted
when you have capital
money
is the common language we can all understand
everywhere across this planet
people pray to god
he never talk back but money talks
so come take a walk with me
let's talk about money
cuz
it makes the world go round
just take a look around you
around the clock we run in circles for the money to purchase all the things
money can buy
all my life
i was taught that money is the root of all evil
but without money how can i feed myself
the same people that say money is evil play the lottery
hoping to win it all
hit the jackpot

since a snot nose
i grew up watching mom gamble for money to buy groceries make scrambled
eggs
praying somebody send a check in the mail
the debt collectors lent us money and they wanted it back

banks don't play about money you gotta pay up!
but with what money?
day and night
working for money but getting nowhere
robbing peter to pay paul
how can you ever progress
if you don't come from money like the top 1%
and instead you trapped with the bottom 99
that's life
when you born poor and can't afford to get sick or pay for a college tuition
why you think i dropped out?
i'm from the bronx
where all you see is crime and poverty
they say new york is where the money is at
but i can't tell
it must have missed us
just look at how we live
like strippers on the pole
how low will you go for the money
when in survival mode
some kill for money
run scams
run up in houses and pull guns out
sell drugs for money cuz with these part time jobs
you aint making no money
paycheck paper thin
that time-money exchange never a fair tradeoff
you can't come up off minimum wage money
that's slave money and master's face is on the bill
in school they taught me how to count numbers and do algebra but how come
they aint say nothing about the mathematics of money?
i always wondered
shit didn't add up so i
started studying the game
reading money manuals to understand the language
assets make money multiply

you can't add hours to the day
pay yourself first
work smart not hard
liabilities divide your money
which side you wanna be on young nigga
would you rather be rich or look rich
following fashion
spending money before you get it
fucking the check up
thinking you'll always get it back
mess up your credit it's hard to get it back
now you got yourself in a hole
im tryna tell you don't nobody know you when you broke
get your money right
the #1 thing to fuck up a marriage is money
money makes your home dysfunctional
don't love nobody hungry for your money
watch for family who only come around when they want something
money and blood don't mix
this is chess not checkers
check yourself and learn to invest money
get real estate
save your money let it gain interest
it's a slow process but what other option do you have
you wanna get off the block or not?
yeah startup money in my sock drawer it's wartime
i'm on the hunt for the money
overtime i hustle to get money like money making mitch rich porter
eye on the prize my mind is on the money
until i get enough money to get this company off the ground
rich radical
laying down the foundation for generations to come
from
a family of jamaicans who came straight off the banana boat
empty handed with no money
imma show you

anything is possible
just wait till i quit my job
move out my mom's house
live out my life the way that i want to i can't wait for the day
i no longer need money
because
money
is just a blank piece of paper
it can't buy meaning

■

work

just got off work and i feel like
every part of my body is hurting
i must be
working too hard
got a splitting headache
aches and pains all over but how can i complain
who else will pay the bills
work to live but this work life is killing me on the inside
what other option do i have?
ever since i was little
i was raised to believe
that in this country
you must work
i come from a family of immigrants
nobody works more than working class poor people
middle class people with kids in little league
but these jobs not working out i need out right now
on the phone with calvin he a working musician
we discussing the algorithm to getting rich
i'm chopping it up with raymond
tryna to figure a way out this wage slavery
the everyday working man's dilemma
that's when you work from sunup to sundown like a machine until you
malfunction
short circuit and can't work anymore
need workers compensation
work day and night
9 to 5
11 to 7
7 to 3 like a sheep fuck sleep work
work
work until the day you retire
ready to die
too tired to fuck when you come home or hug your child

if you wondering where the time went
check the schedule
you spent it working
but somehow the money was never enough to be comfortable
all that work
nothing to show for it but a mortgage
work
work
work
until you short circuit and can't work
your body starts breaking down
you want to break down and cry like a baby
break time
scarf down lunch get back to work
punch the clock
clock in
clock out
like clockwork
work
work
work!
for the money to pay for a place to sleep
sleep 3 or 4 hours then it's up at 3:30 in the morning each morning on the train
dazed and confused like what day is it?
if it's not payday what my day looks like
2 hours both ways to work
splitting headaches aches and pains
every part of my body hurting me
at work
they tell me karl stop daydreaming
we need you to pick up the pace
distant look on my face i'm spaced out and can't pay attention
the paycheck they paying me is playing with my emotions
but it won't be long before i'm gone
man
i know too much

know that
you can work forever and never see your net worth increase
it's like being in the fields
sharecropping
working for free
they freed the slaves
the slaves went back to work for their masters
didn't know no other way than the plantation
modern day
same thing
1 million black men in prison from selling that work
unfit to work
once they come back have to check the box on that job application
you got to be smart or the devil will find work to give you is what granny
always used to tell me
my earliest childhood memories are of seeing her get up and get ready for work
i was tryna help pressing her clothes when i
heard her say i feel old and tired but im on my own and it's no one but me
she 66
still working
it makes me sick
this bullshit must stop!
mom was at work late
i was misbehaving in class
acting out
always thought outside of the box
i aint want to be a doctor or a lawyer but all they tell you in school is get good
grades and go to college so you could get a job and be somebody
our self-worth is connected to where we work at
so when you unemployed you feel worthless like you not worthy of affection
and basic respect
tell me
is that how you measure a man?
by what he has? what work can buy?
buy cars to drive to work
but

why do we work

work

work

what are we working for

is working moving us forward

i wonder what

will happen when robots can do all our jobs faster than we can

without feelings

how's that gonna work

karl!

stop daydreaming

get back to work

we need you to pick up the pace

work faster

why it's always that one asshole at work think you working for him

want to snitch and tattletale to the manager like knuckle don't hurt

and why the fuck am i the only one working?

at

work

work

work

we don't pay you to stand still with your hands in your pockets look busy

we gon put you to work

you got to work

to earn your keep

make a living

live to work

work to make money to pay back debt

rats in a race to the next vacation

running in place for a place to stay

furniture to impress the neighbors

hamsters trapped on a wheel we don't control

for

travel points status symbols carrot stick get back to work

work

work

like a rat
hamsters trapped on a wheel
afraid to face the fact
we can't imagine life without work
but what is it worth if it's purposeless
i
been busy working on a new book
so i could work for myself
purchase investments and make my money work for me
rather be a boss than a worker
it's a lot of work
but little by little i'm working on it because words without work
is not enough and you
get nothing without struggle and hard
work

▪

sick

sitting in a clinic
i'm sick?
sick to my stomach
feeling like my guts is about to spill out
but please sir would u fill out this form
like i don't look sick enough
man
the physician don't give a shit if i live or die
look like
she just here to put me on prescription pills
rushing me through the physical
what's your insurance?
sick
the system is sick and disgusting and i'm sick from the inside out
that's why lately
i aint been eating like that
feel weak and
i can't sleep at night
awake in pain
i stay up tweaking plus
my brain won't keep quiet
all of these
thoughts bounce off the walls
wish i could just crawl into the fetal position and not speak to anybody
know
i need some time to rest
but i gotta get up and go to work
because i get paid by the hour
at work sick
work till i'm sick sick
sick of working
stuck in the middle
still living with my parents
sick from the scent of cigarettes

rented apartment in new york city
where the cost of living
will make you want to run up in somebody crib with a gun and a mask
survival of the fittest
9 million people in competition
these brick walls and paint chips
giving me sick thoughts
sick
sick and i can't think straight or sit still
some days it's a struggle to make it out of bed
with these
headaches and migraines weighing heavy on me
it's been a lot on my mind since i been back home
my whole family been sick
pop won't stop drinking
it's liquor in the fridge but nothing to eat
granny sick
she always sending me to the pharmacy to pick up her medication
every day she put the needle to her veins
when she's in need of an insulin shot
my mama sick
in and out of the hospital like it's going out of style
last time it was 3 o'clock in the morning when the drama started
i heard her scream and call my name
she fell to the floor
help me i'm sick!
quick pick up the phone
was with the paramedics in the back of an ambulance
watching her pass in and out of consciousness
trying to stay calm and not panic
now both of us
so sick it's pathetic
at the ER with all of the rest of the sick people
the things you see be sickening
and if that wasn't enough
the other day they slashed my man in the face

when i saw his scar i was sick
gang initiation
they tried to kill my friend!!
almost hit his jugular vein
shit serious
in the summertime it's a jungle out here
niggas is sick
now everybody on the block
talking about the get back
that's how this bullshit gets started on the boulevard
violence is a vicious cycle
watching it makes me want to cry sometimes i feel helpless
this whole society is sick and psychotic
neurotic
sick white boys walk in with assault weapons and kill everybody
parking lot
middle school
church
university
it doesn't matter
tell me mr. president
what part of the constitution is that?
why am i the one under suspicion
why you picking on the immigrants trying to get into the country?
sick of the racism and inequality
thinking about it makes me sick sick
trying to make it as a young black man in america before a cop shoots me in
the face at point blank range
feel like a mental patient
pacing back and forth
you know what they say about creative people
we bipolar
i don't know you don't get too comfortable
mood swings i'm on the brink
manic depression
i think my mind is starting to slip away

tortured artist
thoughts of giving up i must be sick
insane and crazy
from taking the train seeing addicts with their arms dangling full of tracks
from needle marks
sick of public transportation
last night i saw a man sniffing cocaine up his nose on my way home thought he
was bout to jump on the tracks
sick of not having no money and getting treated like a bitch
sick of this small timing
single sales won't make me a million
sick of minimum wage jobs
it's got to be another option
no matter how impossible it may seem
i can't stop
not now
not because i'm
sick
sick
sick and tired of being tired and sick
broke as a bitch
sitting the bench
i think it's time for a change
just wait
till i get back right
all of my enemies gon be
sick!

■

niggas are scared of revolution

niggas
are scared
of revolution
but niggas shouldn't be scared of revolution because revolution is nothing but
change and all niggas do is change
their hair from red to black to blue purple and blond
hoping that their looks will change
hopeless niggas exchange drugs for money on the avenue to make quick change
frustrated from long days of work at jobs that will never pay enough
niggas just say fuck it and give up on trying to change their circumstances
come home from work
change into boxer drawers
sit on the couch with a six pack
change the channel and laugh at commercials
when it's game time niggas
can't take their eyes off the screen
niggas place bets and yell at the television
watching other niggas play football
baseball and basketball while white supremacy is cutting off their balls
niggas pay more attention to ball players than they play with their daughters
and sons or pay in child support niggas support sports teams more than they
believe in each other
crabs in a bucket niggas root for you to fail
i wonder what is the root cause of the issue
niggas
treat women like dogs
barking orders
at their baby mamas
wives and girlfriends
calling them bitches
being disrespectful
but depend on them bitches when the rent is due
to pay the bills
make food and wash their clothes but

niggas
don't seem to be capable of staying faithful
but niggas always seem to need a place to stay
niggas are ungrateful
confront a nigga
niggas play dumb because niggas are players
everything is a game to niggas
but niggas play too much
toy with her heart
she get fed up change the lock on the doors
niggas say please baby
i was just playing don't put me out
i'll change
niggas always putting females through bullshit changes
you make the mistake of taking him back find out his act was just a put on
next thing you know that nigga putting his hands on you
damn
it was all good in the beginning
when did niggas change?
niggas switch phones change names and addresses
niggas change their hair from red to purple blue and blond
posted on the block
posing for pictures with silly captions
fishing for attention can i get a hug ass niggas
change their outfits
several times a day
outside on the bench all day so you could admire the fit
but don't look too hard
hard niggas find it hard to fill out job applications
when niggas
can't adapt to changes in the economy
new technology makes
niggas obsolete
niggas don't know how to act in public places
niggas always overreacting
acting out at the cookout

spazzing
over nothing
demanding respect because they can't get it for anything
that's actually important
niggas cut up faces at house parties and shoot up clubs

niggas follow the code of the street but don't know that won't pay for the
stroller or buy groceries

niggas think they're so fucking cute
you step on a nigga's shoes watch him threaten to fuck you up
the question is when will niggas step to the real enemy?
i'm just keeping it real niggas
niggas love to talk about keeping it real
but most of what niggas think of as being real is real dumb
for real niggas
see you reading a book
and ask what's that?
niggas laugh and make fun of you
you try to become better

young niggas don't let niggas discourage you

don't believe half of what you see and none of what you overhear
think for yourself find out what's real
most of these niggas tryna be cartoons
skin peeling i could see the concealer
plastic peeling foundation clay mask
you an act nigga!

uh

niggas don't know the meaning of the word real
really to be honest

niggas are scared of revolution

but not afraid to kill each other for little to nothing so many niggas die
from violence but more niggas die
from white carbs and carcinogens
cigarettes nicotine liquor the whole nine
white sugar
diabetes
niggas been fed a lie
eating it like monkey banana
they should've never let you niggas have money
niggas get famous and move to hollywood
lose their minds and change into buffoons
saying shit like things have changed
slavery was a choice
racism it no longer exists and you middle class niggas think it's true
you got a little job
they gave you a position in the big house
in 2008 we elected a black president
niggas celebrated like it was juneteenth
it's a new day niggas thought
change had finally come to america but a decade later
niggas thinking they thought wrong
it's starting to dawn on niggas
nothing has changed
it's still a million niggas in prison
millions more under supervision of courts
on probation and parole whole families of niggas
fucked up and dysfunctional
communities fractured
cities of black people
no clean water
schools without heat in the winter
white police killing niggas like it's target practice
at the corner store in broad daylight
at stop lights
license and registration
it was a routine regular traffic stop until the cop popped one in his face and the

nigga stopped breathing
right in front of his wife and child

niggas got it on tape
cop get off scotch free
blame it on the red tape

niggas talk about civil rights like those exist for niggas
they tryna extinguish all niggas

from the looks of it it's beginning to look like america has changed its mind
when will niggas get the message
they dont give a fuck about us it's no justice
it's up to niggas to take change into their own hands no man can wave his hands and do that for us niggas need to stop sitting on their hands but who am i kidding
i know its niggas sitting in the audience right now listening to this wishing i'd change the subject

niggas quiet!
i think i hit a nerve
really i think an atomic bomb hit niggas like nagasaki
they stripped us of our names and started calling us niggas
stole our land
robbed us of our language
self-confidence customs and ways of life
chained us to the bottom of ships named jesus and mary and with the blessing of the church
father son and holy spirit forced us to work for free for hundreds of years
nigga
till the field
pick the cotton
sugar cane and tobacco
put your back into it nigga
chop that timber

work in the mines and mind their children
at the dinner table
don't speak nigga mind your manners
fight and die in our wars
financed by banks that wouldn't give niggas a loan to become
home owners
niggas
used to build universities
now
niggas wipe windows
sweep floors and wait on tables downtown

wait in the kitchen there's company
the masters of civilization
disenfranchised and systematically excluded
lynched at picnics and hung from trees is how they did niggas if niggas tried to
resist
think twice you blink or cough in the presence of a white woman
violent mobs with pitchforks
knives
and burning crosses on the lawns of homes of niggas
just trying to live with signs saying no niggers allowed
loud and clear they locked out niggas
redlined and confined niggas to the poor section and designated it the ghetto
niggas cried out and rioted
they hit niggas with crack
assassinated all the leaders tryna teach niggas that's how they keep niggas like
sheep
why niggas separate and unequal
today an endangered species on the verge of extinction niggas like exotic birds

in the absence of leadership all niggas got is a circus of niggas
who don't do nothing but sing songs
and dance like clowns
clown ass niggas build platforms made out of paper
mache niggas don't stand for nothing

tap dancing just to get a fanbase
from rapping
but don't say nothing but
nigga
nigga
nigga
niggas ego tripping on that bullshit
niggas
need a different framework
a change of perspective
old ways not working
it's a different time

niggas envision
a future

it's no easy solution

no nigga has all the answers but niggas are afraid to ask questions
because niggas have been conditioned
spayed and neutered
domesticated like house cats
too pussy to
challenge the status quo
ask me why i care
talk so harsh and criticize niggas
because
i'm a nigga too
that's why
i love niggas
give a fuck about niggas
because i come from niggas
was raised by niggas
live with niggas
family full of niggas
what will happen to my little niggas

if niggas don't get it together
i said it before and i'll say it again
niggas
are scared of revolution

visionary

speak about things before they happen
words are magnetic
imagination manifests dreams
speak about my present in the past tense
like i can see the future
genius level talent
passion and ambition
wisdom inspiration and shit talking for you on the pursuit of happiness
raw facts and unadulterated truth
what you've come to expect from the author
where i'm from not too many niggas like me come along
one in a million
it'll never be another one like me i'm hard to find
who reinvented the wheel?
got it lit like electricity
nikola tesla
electrical shock on the block
who brought the bronx back put it back on the map map
i swear none of these niggas out
even on my planet!
fuck the competition
i'm just being honest speaking me truth
i aint got to lie
the story i'm telling compelling enough by itself
i could sell sand to the seashore
like a real new york nigga
prepare for landing
young
rich
radical
with the distribution deal
we integrated vertically baby
middle finger parental advisory sticker
listen kid don't tell your parents you're listening to me before you drop out of

school
they run and say k did it
bitch
excuse me
clear the runway i got money to make
the plane is about to take off
thousands of miles above sea level
having visions in the clouds
executive suite i guess you could say i elevated my level
in the elevator laughing with the cameraman an accountant and an attorney
the journey is worth more than the destination but you could bet by the end of it
my net worth won't even make no sense
young
rich
radical
visionary living legend
put that in the papers and print it
let the record reflect
a nigga came a long way
watch the hometown kid
come back and build a school for the children
sit back enjoy the fruits of my labor
roots run deep through the city like the expressway
they said i was crazy
didn't believe me but i did it
speak things into existence before they happen
words are magnetic
imagination manifests dreams
speak about the present in past tense like i can see the future
visionary
the world is mine

■

synthesizer

what's your addiction?
is it prescription pills porn or purple syrup?
cups of coffee
liquor
nicotine
marijuana
cocaine
opioids
smartphones
android or iphone?
tell me
what's the difference?
world at your fingertips
twitching
itching and scratching
for a quick hit of that dopamine shot to the brain
tryna catch up to that first high
doesn't it feel like magic?
you tell yourself to stop but you keep scrolling
begging please
synthesizer
feed me i need a fix
doubt i ever leave my house without it in my pocket
purse
jacket check
keys check
wallet check
verified check
see the blue light light up the screen
feel it vibrate
that's when the feeling starts eating at you
that's when you reach for it
every night it sleeps besides you
hooked like a fish on the line

hook
line
and sinker
swimming through a sea of media mostly meaningless information
but i'm attached and handcuffed
attracted to it like a magnet doesn't it feel magical?
know it's doing damage to my attention but man this shit is habit forming just
like crack
you can't kick it
you gotta have it have it now
if not you might have an anxiety attack
where is it
you start panicking
xanax over the counter
can't sit at the dinner table with family and friends without
counting down the seconds and minutes
check for a text message every few minutes
it's an everyday struggle trying to stay unplugged
sometimes it's hard to fucking function
synthesizer
wire me up
i'm uninspired
make me feel better
i can't get enough
update me to the latest news
what did the president say today?
upload me when i feel lonely
i don't wanna be alone
i wanna be liked
i need love
refresh to see how many more
i wanna be down
repost me
retweet
i wanna be seen
overstimulated fiending for validation

don't ever need to be bored
send me a screenshot
a perfect snapshot of life
i wanna be just like that
tell me have you ever seen someone tap his veins with a needle?
start nodding off sleepwalking
because i see zombies walk down the street eyes glued to the screen like
nothing else seems to matter
unlimited high speed data connection...
still disconnected
possessed by technology
body appendage
when there's autocorrect you don't need to know how to spell
why read?
the internet tells me everything i need to know in an instant
much quicker
quick hit me i can't sit still!
ping notification
internet niggas get famous hiding behind a fake persona and in the hood if they want to book you all they got to do is look at your facebook you putting it all out there bunch of weirdos posting pictures of drugs guns and money like it's
all fun and games
but the police know your location
the phone company sold you out
your mobile device is connected to a tower in the sky
that mic is always on
even when the power is off so watch what you talking because the court of
public opinion is listening
yeah
big data is the new big brother
we been hacked by the clever algorithms of computer programmers in silicon
valley!
look at you
your fingertips is twitching right now
palms itching
arms scratching

keep it within arm's reach
eyes glued to the screen
even the babies is hypnotized by the microwave
not paying attention to the teacher
they don't play outside anymore
why read or learn how to spell?
the internet tells me everything i need to know
computer
digitize me into a byte sized
sound bite
pry into my private life
make me feel like i'll live forever
i wanna be liked
i need you right now in an instant quick
fix me
give me positive feedback make me feel better when i'm frustrated
and overanxious
serve me
over the counter
upload me when i feel down
i wanna be down
don't want to be left out
thanks to you
i never have to be bored
tell me
what's your affliction?
is it netflix?

prescription pills
opioids
smartphone
android
iphone
heroin tell me what is the difference? it's dope all the same
they just remix it
whole world at your fingertips

twitching itching and scratching for a hit
double click
shot to the brain
you try to break the spell but can't shake the monkey
drugs to a fiend
syringe needle
fiending for attention scrolling your feed
synthesizer
please feed me
i need you
don't ever leave me sleep beside me don't know if i can be in this life without
you
out of focus
unhinged and out of touch
double tap
don't forget to tag me
wash
rinse
recycle
repost
retweet
repeat
feedback
synthesizer i need you
please feed me

∎

rich

twinkle in my eye
an itch that i can't scratch
picture maps and affirmations on my wall
mattress still on the floor
scratching off the days on the calendar
till i escape this animal planet
jungle habitat full of piranhas
young visionary on a mission i didn't ask for permission
so sit your ass down and be quiet
underprivileged
i'm from the underbelly of the inner city
was born poor
so i simply cannot afford to sit on my hands and live with my parents
i got bigger plans
college dropout they didn't gimme a scholarship
skipped class to sell a book of poetry that i wrote and published when i was
only eighteen years old with no hair on my face
was sitting in my dorm room counting money adding up mathematics
plastic wrap on the paperback books
volume 2 cooking up
looks like we back at it again
but remember when i'd had enough
got tired of folding polo shirts making $11 dollars an hour
so i
quit that job and didn't give two weeks' notice
went to go see the plug
and started a clothing brand from a black duffel bag
new york hustler
walk my dogs
talk with an accent
bronx savage
nomad
cowboy hat
black leather jacket

i don't have shit for the establishment but a parental advisory sticker and the middle finger
finnah get rich without a lottery ticket
they didn't pick me for valedictorian but
gimme a pack to flip and i'll be back in a few with a few hundred
creative asset straight from the manufacturer
no little man in the middle
handshakes at the bank
i'm laughing!
plan
plot
strategize
i chop syllables for my spinach and pop shit
one man pop up shop
popping up on you with product
i got it out the mud
watching the words
lock up in the pot
whipping this fortune 500 forbes list
i said it!
how else you set destiny in motion?
don't want nobody to give me nothing i get it myself
and
if i spot an opportunity it's only one option
run up to the side of his car stick my hand through the window!
stop
the traffic
drop the mic if they disrespect my name
i'm reckless
renegade always ready for war
aggressive set tripping on investments
that's how we
gangbanging in the 21st century
cuz we
too talented to stand in front of the building trapping it's too many cameras
don't fall for the trap!

tapping into a new level
well respected and connected
all over the country
tryna do it independent like master p in the 90s
gimme 85 percent i takeover the game like jay-z
just watch me
sick wid it like e-40 in the parking lot pop the trunk
got a way with words that'll make me a rich
multi-millionaire
true capitalist adam smith
build businesses
get rich
give it back
start a school to spark minds
fly out the country to have lunch
see myself in a young nigga
put the game on his brain
you aint got to be a drug dealer to make money
use your imagination
i could show you the tools of the trade
teach you how to speak the language
reveal the secrets
you got to speak it into existence
for it to happen you gotta see it first
you don't gotta believe me see for yourself
seize the time
believe that you are valuable
a genius
that's how we did it
now picture maps and affirmations on my wall
plan
plot
strategize buy the blocks
cop the properties
reinvest and repeat
until we all rich
that's the vision!

radical

kick in the door
stick the word to your temple

uh !

point blank range
deliver the message
period. point. blank.
put your brains on the doormat
this aint your average everyday
ladies and gentlemen
the king is here to claim his throne
take a seat
watch as i
take my place in the pages of history
make waves and declare my greatness
karl with a k

make sure you spell it right
say the whole thing
no exceptions

intelligent rebel living legend
public enemy #1 when a pen is in my hand
i state phrases that make
men tremble in fear
plain and simple

pistol whip an ignorant mind
strip you naked
of all that brainwashing
make your beliefs shake bitch
shift your paradigm

explode your limited thinking
expose the facade like socrates
rebel ready to set it off
explosive like a grenade set to detonate
spark
the revolution from a blank piece of paper
take it to the extreme like john brown
jimi hendrix broken guitar
john coltrane on the sax

passionate like tupac
makaveli in the booth
speak the truth
spit the facts

i'm not a rapper i'm a radical
richard wright meets richard branson
about that action like george jackson and the black panthers until the crackers
strap me to the chair

play with language like piano keys
black sheep
i was the family disappointment
because i didn't graduate
wasn't paying attention to the teacher

what a waste of potential is what i heard them tell me
i was skipping class to sell paperback books
invest in myself
build a brand
get established
you pussy ass internet niggas wouldn't understand me
i wasn't handed a penny
and since
they murdered
my african ancestors on the plantation

i can't find it in me to stand for the national anthem or salute the flag
rebellion is in my dna

bronx accent
at the sit down
walk with purpose
talk with conviction
7
8
digits the minimum that's not a figure of speech
we talking
real estate
publishing
music and fashion
stand on stage like a man possessed

on the rooftop of my building
i saw a starry night
that's when god called me and told me to be a leader
not a follower
so what if dumb people make fun of me ?
fuck em all
say it with my chest out
speak out
stick out like a sore thumb
i'm from the gutter where they don't accept you when you know how to spell
why learn how to read when you not expected to be nothing
remember i came into this world
premature with a hole in my chest
yet here i stand
a testimony
to a living miracle

kick in the door
let these words stick to your temple
pay close attention
i got a story to tell

special

hey there little chocolate drop
stop
let me talk to you for a minute
may i ask you a question?
do i have your permission?
body the shape of an hourglass
you got a mind that's captivating
you walked past me and time stopped
to be honest i forgot myself
in conversation you
say things that catch my attention
can't get you out of my head
i must admit
since the first time i ever saw you you been all i can think about
come chill with a radical
sit on my lap
let me tell you a story
what you think about being friends?
it could be something special
i've met hundreds of women but none as special as you
let me know
let me know
cuz i'll let you know from the introduction what i'm about i've got nothing to hide
fuck the text messages
i want to talk to you face to face
let's send letters back and forth
i'll get it to you when you least expect it
check your mailbox
i sent it special delivery
keep it between us so it's special
send roses to your door
take you out
show you off

don't be shy
come
hold my hand
tell me about your plans dreams goals and aspirations
you so smart and ambitious
i love to listen to you
it's a lot i believe we could teach each other
it's a lot in this life to see
places we could go
let's make a list
i promise i won't waste your time and i hope you give me the same respect
let's take our time make this
special

hey there
back to you
pretty ass caramel queen
i been daydreaming
did you miss me?
we both been busy working
you handle your business on your own and don't need me
but you tell me you don't always want to have to be strong
that's why you run into my arms and call me daddy
knew we would happen
it was just a matter of timing
i been patient
waiting for the day i could cradle your body in my hands as if you was a
newborn baby
helpless and naked
when you with me you could be yourself there's no need in being afraid
lay down and relax
aint nobody else here
it's been a long time since i've last seen you
i'm tryna see about you
stretch out your legs
let me tell you a story

i been wanting to flex you in different positions
get you dripping wet
whisper poetry in your ear
strip you down
rip your clothes off with my teeth
close your eyes
i got the blindfold
tie your hands with my bandana
you don't know what's happening
don't be so surprised
i already told you i'm an animal
tap you till your eyes roll back
i thought i told you
i'd rather show you than tell you
i don't have nothing else left to say
let's take our time
make this
special

transition

candles lit the curb
the whole neighborhood lit
you aint heard it on the news?
late last night
on the block
it was a murder
word is
he got kilt
in the back alley of my building
savage animals burnt him to a black crisp in the backseat of a stolen
vehicle
just to send a message now the witnesses scared to snitch on who did it
transition
the next day i couldn't pay attention to the teacher
what's a christopher columbus
it's nervous tension in my body
from the
homicides in my zip code
i tried to play it off
hoping nobody would notice but really i was just playing pretend acting out
i was just playing but they suspended me
labeled me a problem
transition to a fiend
getting beaten to a bloody pulp in front of me
dealer asking
where my money at
you better
have it for me
transition
yellow tape faces on t-shirts and posters
i wonder do you know where your children been
in an abandoned building
taking laced blunts to the face getting wasted
chilling in the park

drinking
hard liquor
thinking they're grown
don't they know it all
swimming with the sharks
playing with fire
trying to get fly like the vultures
skipping class
picking locks
it's all fun and games
until somebody get locked up
they get a little older
get put on to the set
transition to home invasions and weighing grams on the scale
hate to break it to you but they might probably get life
before they make it to graduation
plus my little man making the same mistakes
he more than his mom can handle
hanging loose from a vine
swinging in the jungle with monkeys and gorillas
no matter how hard i tried i could not get through to him
my desperate attempts was useless
transition
im sorry mam
there's nothing we could do about it
your son has gone missing
he vanished
disappeared into the back of that van
niggas kidnapped and executed him gangland style
like wild cowboys
with no conscience
transition
my upbringing in the bronx was violent
picture with me
humble beginnings
without a silver spoon living in the hood with no cable or wifi

quarters nickels and dimes hand to my mouth
hands praying to god for a straight path to the transition
lost in the wilderness without a map it was never fair
me and my granny
had to split sandwiches standing under the rain
wonder do anybody really care for us
stuck in them tenements
in the grey sky sometimes
it's hard
to see a silver lining
under the poverty line scraping the bottom of the pot with a knot in my
stomach
nothing but lint in my pockets i could not find a crystal staircase to deliver me
but
still i climbed
transition
still i rise because
being resilient is in my dna
forced to figure out my place in this jigsaw puzzle of life
without the guidance of a father figure i'm surprised i made it here
self-made entrepreneur
in transition out the sewage
thinking i needed to see a shrink
because every time i thought about my childhood all i could see was birthdays i
spent laying in bed staring up at the ceiling
numb
doing nothing
frustrated with no money to spend or a friend to call
once upon a time
times was different
all friendly
i was happy go lucky
a funny guy
always cracking jokes
transition to an adolescent
why is it now

i don't smile as much?
could it be
my spirit has been touched by poison
bodies cut up in the dumpster
having bad dreams of
being murdered
will i die young?
i don't know
the fights and police sirens in the street make it hard to sleep at night
i was 12 years old
up at 5:30 early in the morning making a breakfast
plain bread and butter
taking myself to school on the train
but i wasn't buying
what they were trying to sell me
all the textbooks do is tell lies
falsify my history
transition
this was the beginning of my self-education
the start of my commitment to this discipline
of whipping words
wrist twisting since 16
taking risks and chances to get established
this transition is religious to me
writing on walls therapeutic
misunderstood
i had a vision nobody understood but me
they dismissed me as crazy
i couldn't fit in but i didn't want to
guess that's why
they didn't pick me first
i picked myself
walking through the hallway
saying affirmations to raise my self-esteem i had to be a
self starter
my block offered me no solutions

and no
i wasn't doing nothing
but my pop still put his hands on me for no reason
angry my hands balled into a fist
all i could see was a sea of red
livid
spitting out curse words
kicking over furniture
mad enough to flip the living room table
kiss my ass
you make me sick to my stomach
sick to my stomach on the verge of a nervous breakdown
shaking and crying
sticking up my middle finger
transition!
city marshal standing in the doorway
with a police officer a padlock and an eviction notice to kick us outdoors
rough life but i'd become immune to it you got to tough it out
but underneath
i was suffering inside
transition putting me through changes
relationship with my mother crumbling into pieces
in pieces with ink stains on my fingertips i think i'll put it in between the pages
of my diary
document the different phases of life
for the ones that's like
now can you believe it
my diary became a book
look now
i sold over 1,000!
ask me how
i transitioned
from thanksgiving dinner with no electricity
can't see the fork i'm eating with
shivering in the frigid cold
refrigerator naked

ducking
paint chips from the ceiling
i couldn't take it
told myself i wouldn't
stand for this misery any longer
do you understand
where i'm coming from?
it comes a time
when a man must stand upright
when challenged by adversity
in transition
difficult circumstances
activated my animal instincts
stick your chest out and handle it
it's all a process of transformation
progress of a metamorphosis
transition
college didn't pan out so now
i'm with the pen and the paper
young and ambitious
i
stick to my guns
imma make it my way
at the table politicking on how to make more
fatigue bandana around my forehead
out late nights
with the duffel bag for my stripes
grinding
under the bridge by the highway
in a city
200 miles away from my home on my way to make a sale
always in transition
the kid make it look like it's magic
mastered this craft
passion is contagious
it magnetizes the money to me

true stories based on my interactions with random strangers
transactions exchanging paperbacks made them into paying customers
hand to hand to establish a platform
i was born without access
activated at any place
any time
you liable to find me
in the middle of the street with the people lined up in a circle
mesmerized by my style of expression
transition
making flips one after the other then another one
double back a couple more
re-up on a new package and get back to it pinch every penny then reinvest
real estate developments in my field of interest
forbes list on my checklist
intelligent menace to the white supremacist system
transition i traffic language to overcome the trap of being a young black man in america under a corrupt vicious political system designed to put me in a prison cell but statistics will not predict my future
you cannot stop me
it's impossible
i am not your typical
refuse
to be denied
never consent to a narrative of my own victimization
transition
unconventional
my eyes see through the plot
man of conviction
prepared to die by my principles in the line of fire for my beliefs
even if it costs me my life
i will define myself
surround myself with radicals
militant thinkers in my inner circle
activists
artists

lawyers
scientists business owners and musicians
transition
i laid the building blocks
paved the foundation to make my name
built a community from nothing
transition now you see me on the top floor of the office building in meetings
with executives and directors
devils cannot extinguish my fire colonize my mind or silence my voice
compromise my ideas
transition
visionary by any means necessary
it's just me and my brother david
since day one
my man anthony
my brother
kamau been with me since sneaking in through the window
my sister been with me since the beginning
been in the cut with raphael on deck with the camera
calvin on production
yeah
white man had a script written for us we ripped it up and burnt it
his master plan backfired
master of my fate in command of my enterprise
young niggas in transition like slaves on the underground railroad it's no way
back
minimum wage is no life at all
you might as well be dead
transition
on the park bench next to the projects
in the trenches with the welfare recipients
on the curb with the mexicans
incarcerated ex convicts
harriet tubman with a pistol
disruptive like frederick douglass in his prime
richard branson

david walker
author
slash
outlaw
on a mission
to transition
into a boss
rich radical from the bronx
consider that written
in stone

.

what's free?

what's free?
free is when nobody can tell me what to be
when i can stand on my own two feet
finally
financially free
and don't need a job
sharecropping
basically
working for free
but you tell me
what's free if it's just me?

and still no justice
for the millions of my people locked up behind bars
caged like animals
not free
living in poverty without clean water
not enough to eat
in the so-called "land of the free"
feel like
our basic needs should be free
but the greed of "free"-market capitalist corporations
keeps the country so divided and unequal

plus incarceration is obsolete
all political prisoners deserve to be set free
they was only trying to teach us that freedom is not free
it's a constant struggle but
you motherfuckers don't know what's free
wall street cheat you out your home get off scot free
IRS take over 20% of your check every week while the top 1% practically
living tax free
drone strikes overseas in the 21st century
death is now dealt hands free

hands up don't shoot!

another black child found dead in the street
everybody on
social media
while his killer still alive whistling dixie walking around carefree as can be
we should've tossed his body off the freeway if you ask me!
but i'm in my feelings
fuck the supreme court
cuz it's never been for us but that's just me
exercising my freedom of speech
some cats claim they wanna be free
but really just wish they could bleach they skin white
i tell it like it is that's why sellout niggas dislike me
why that university didnt give me a scholarship
but im not tripping
imma still get rich
independent like master p
so no printing press can pimp me
my thoughts are expensive
you wanna talk to me it's gon cost you
if you not talking bout a revolution why you even bother to call me?

published author who would've thought?
poetry saved my life real talk and
reading decolonized my imagination

i started writing for free

never thought people would pay me for it
it's crazy what you can become when you let your mind be free
but honestly
i won't be happy till i can see my granny stress free
tell her you can come home now kick your feet up baby
we debt free
i built a company

and didn't have to stand out in front of the building selling drugs
entrepreneur
free to do what i want
but for now
it's all just a big dream
because i find myself still
stuck in the mud and under pressure
living through this oppression
wishing i knew what it feels like to be free
you feel me?

∎

beautiful struggle

nightmares in broad daylight with my eyes wide open
only if
this was
just a dream
aunty got cancer screaming she's dying
all times of the night
difficult to deal with i must admit
living this way

sometimes i get discouraged

in my quiet moments i spend alone
feeling like
nobody really understands my ambition
this radical i got inside of me
but i can't afford to see a psychologist anymore
so i write down
in between the sheets of my diary
all these feelings
i otherwise
would never get the chance to express
sometimes i get discouraged
cuz
sickness
misery
ignorance and death
surround me on all sides when i step outside
yes i'm busy trying to break the cycle
but any time i try to change for the better
it's my own people that stand in my way
everytime …
only child
watching my own mother deteriorate
squinting her eyes like she's going blind

on all types of medication
wishing she'd find a way to shake the weight off and maybe come up off those
motherfucking cigarettes cuz lately
we been trading places in hospital beds like it's a game of musical chairs
plus my father stares at me like he wanna push me off the planet
we exchange hate

sometimes i get discouraged

tired from all the thinking and planning
mapping my way out of this maze
counting down dog days
frustrated frothing at the mouth
from bad breaks and the setbacks common to a young black male
not knowing when it will happen for me
watching all these dumb rappers play monkey for the camera
doing numbers on the billboard
i guess the crackers not interested in your story unless you live in the projects
sell drugs and represent a set
i got to question why is that they don't want us to be intelligent?
but in the meantime
you could find me
still grinding
on the street selling paperbacks of special k
far away from any media attention
sleeping on a mattress in the basement waiting for my day to come
on the pavement trying to make my way
cuz I got something to say so why should i lie down and be quiet?
i'm no choir boy with his nose in the bible
i'm more of the type to start the fire
write words to spark your mind
feel like my purpose in life is to be like the light from a candle in the dark
or that distant voice telling you that it'll be alright when you can't see past your
challenges
sometimes i get discouraged but I still get up
stick my chest out to the test and give my best to it

bring my guts to it to get through trying times
trials and tribulations
remember that faith is the bridge over troubled waters when you get
discouraged
because i know i do
so i'm just here to remind y'all
that the
struggle itself
is
beautiful

.

tribute to the bronx

look past the garbage
over the trains and
under the expressway
where they overlook
look through the pollution
in between the crowded avenues and busy streets
there you'll see it's the city of the bronx new york
the place where I came of age
oh you not familiar?
haven't been past 125th
well if that's the case come take a trip with me
lemme show you what it's all about so you could see just how we live
so you could see the blacks and puerto ricans
dominicanos italianos and chicanos
immigrants from many different places in this great melting pot
the strips malls and car washes
liquor stores and pawn shops
children with limited opportunities
not enough options
frustrated in poverty
people pushing bottles and cans in shopping carts to the supermarket
for nickels dimes and quarters
trying to make dollars
junkies and alcoholics strung out
lying face down on the hot concrete
homeless and broken hearted off that
empty
broken
vial needles
syringes
in veins
numb the pain of a fiend who was once fat but now skinny
eyes seen too much
what a pitiful sight to see her digging in the trash

arguments and fights outside every night
families beefing with slumlords
for some heat in the winter when it's freezing
hardworking single mamas on ebt running hard not to miss the bus
absentee papas missing in action
where they at?
aunties uncles and cousins under one roof all on top of each other sons
sitting behind prison walls
daughters pregnant before their time
tenement fires so many innocent lives lost
behind the building
knock knock it's a raid
killer coppers chasing robbers killers drug dealers
it seems to be the
only time the news and helicopters come
seldom seen
politicians only come around when it's election time tryna play us like we
dumb
racist institutions won't fix our roads or fund our schools
they say we useless
too ghetto
won't ever amount to much of nothing
so what's the sense in educating people made to slave in the kitchen
take orders
sweep floors and drive cabs for the rich people on madison avenue?
huh animal habitat picture that
it's like a jungle sometimes
a constant struggle just to get by
summertimes surviving off cold cuts from the corner bodega
wondering if i was gon make it or go under because
i'm up to my neck in it
so don't push me
close to the edge
trying to clear my headspace and make sense of it all
as I walk down the street and take a look around me
not a bookstore in sight

nowhere to buy groceries of fresh produce but we got the most green space in
the whole new york
youth hopeless with no signs that say out
they say we too ghetto
won't ever amount to much of nothing
but what the hell those gringos know about our borough
home of the thoroughbred and the talented
where all this hip-hop got started
before it went pop and lost its spark
we tagged our names in graffiti
so they could see us
because we was invisible
back when power from the streetlights made the place dark
spinning on cardboard at the park jams
stop the violence but ya'll must've forgot about that
when they wrote
us off
left us out and gave us no choice
we made something from nothing
let me tell you a little something about where i'm from
because you don't know nothing!
pelham parkway is where i came of age
so make that a historic landmark
not too far away from arthur avenue and the botanical gardens one of the
largest in the world
where roses grow from concrete
bet you aint know that
genius is hidden in the cracks
of despair
if you open your eyes to see
past the garbage
look at the architecture that lines the grand concourse
i'm here to let you know its more to it than Yankee Stadium
in the BX US of A
the place to be if you need a fresh trim from the barbershop call me
where you got to stop at if you want to get your ethnic food authentic

to top it all off like chopped cheese in the Bronx
home to some of the most genuine people you'll ever meet
guaranteed
we got bright minds
scientists
artists
and if you aint know now you know
the greatest poet of our time is a local!
yeah
I left to get it crackin in DC but you know i had to come back
to be an ambassador
put us back on the map map and give back
to the blocks that gave me my game
made me raise cain and abel to
carve my name in legend and represent
open up shop and buy properties
cuz
honestly we like the last ones left
one of the few places in the empire state
they have yet to gentrify
we can't just lie down and let em take it from us push us out
nah
it's up to us
to make em put some respect on our name
no obstacle is impossible to overcome
if we come together
stop the bickering and the fighting
stand up to lay claim to the greatness of our city
make our home a better place

if we use our imagination
i have a dream
we can change

Author Bio

Karl Omar Lawrence is a poet and social entrepreneur from the Bronx, New York. He began writing at the age of 11 years old and has been performing his work ever since he was a teenager. He is a passionate believer in the power that words have to transform people and inspire change in our society. Visit his website at richradical.com for more information on new project releases, music, videos and live performances.

www.ingramcontent.com/pod-product-compliance
Lightning Source LLC
Chambersburg PA
CBHW051411290426
44108CB00015B/2238